The Financial Compass
Navigating a Course to Secure Your Future

Andrew Galowey

Copyright © [Andrew Galowey] [2024]. All rights reserved. No part of this publication may be reproduced, distributed, or transmitted in any form or by any means, including photocopying, recording, or other electronic or mechanical methods, without the prior written permission of the publisher, except in the case of brief quotations embodied in critical reviews and certain other noncommercial uses permitted by copyright law.

Table Of Contents

Introduction

Chapter 1: Charting Your Course: Setting Financial Goals and Creating Your Roadmap

Chapter 2: Understanding Your Financial Landscape: Budgeting, Cash Flow, and Net Worth

Chapter 3: Weathering Storms: Risk Management and Protecting Your Future

Chapter 4: Investing for Growth: Selecting the Best Tools and Strategies

Chapter 5: Life's Adventures: Making Big Financial Decisions

Chapter 6: Maintaining Your Course: Monitoring Progress, Re-evaluating, and Making Changes

Introduction

Have you ever been adrift at sea, uncertain of your path or destination? This is how it might feel to navigate your money without a strategy. The future might be unpredictable, and financial choices can be difficult. But what if you had a reliable advisor, a "Financial Compass," who could steer you in the correct way and help you plan a route for a secure future?

This book is your guide to financial literacy and empowerment. In these pages, you'll discover how to create clear objectives, manage financial storms, make good investment decisions, and adjust your strategy when life throws curveballs. "The Financial Compass" will provide you the information and confidence you need to take charge of your financial future via practical tactics and simple explanations. Set sail with us on this adventure and experience the tranquil seas of financial stability.

Chapter 1: Charting Your Course: Setting Financial Goals and Creating Your Roadmap

Imagine you are at the helm of a ship. The wide ocean spreads out before you, an unending expanse of possibilities. However, without a goal in mind, a path planned, and a compass to guide you, this freedom may rapidly become overpowering. The same is true for your money. Navigating the financial waters might be difficult if you don't have clear objectives and a well-defined strategy.

your chapter acts as your first companion on your financial journey. We'll provide you the skills you need to define significant financial objectives, both short and long term, and then turn those goals into a tailored road map for success.

Setting Sail with Goals: Where Would You Like to Go?

The first step in every trip is to identify your goal. What do you see for your financial future? Do you want to be a homeowner, retire comfortably, or go on a dream vacation? Perhaps your ambitions are more personal: paying for your child's school, establishing a company, or just having piece of mind knowing you have a financial safety net.

Financial objectives come in all forms and sizes. However, the most successful objectives have a few common characteristics:

- Specificity: Vague goals such as "having more money" lack focus. Aim for specific objectives, such as "saving $10,000 for a down payment on a house within two years."
- Measurability: How will you know you've met your goal? Define success using unambiguous measurements. Instead of just "saving for retirement,"

establish a retirement savings goal and a schedule for achieving it.
- Attainability: While desire is important, make sure your objectives are achievable given your present financial condition. A million dollars next year may be an unreasonable goal, but saving $500 every month is a good place to start.
- Relevancy: Match your aims to your values and priorities. Is financial security your first priority, or are you ready to take measured risks to retire early?
- Time-bound: Set a deadline for your objectives to help you feel more motivated and focused.

Goal Setting in Action: A Case Study

Let us assume Sandra, a young professional with a consistent salary. She hopes to explore the globe for a year after five years. This broad intention may be converted into a precise, quantifiable, and achievable objective.

- Goal: Save $30,000 over five years to fund a year-long travel excursion.
- Measurable: Use a designated savings account to track progress and check the amount on a regular basis.
- Attainable: Research typical trip expenses and adjust your funds appropriately. Consider Sandra's income and current spending when calculating a reasonable monthly savings amount.
- Relevant: Traveling is a vital value for Sandra's, and this aim reflects her enthusiasm for adventure and discovery.
- Time-bound: The five-year period sets a specific goal date.

Creating Your Financial Roadmap: From Dreams to Action

With your objectives clearly in sight, it's time to turn them into a concrete strategy. Here's the navigation toolbox:

- Budgeting is the foundation of every financial plan. Track your income and spending to see where your money goes. Several budgeting strategies exist, including the 50/30/20 rule (which allocates 50% to necessities, 30% to desires, and 20% to savings and debt reduction). Choose an approach that works for you and stay with it.
- Savings Strategy: Determine how much you can actually save each month to achieve your objectives. Consider setting up automatic transfers from your checking account to a high-yield savings account to help you develop the habit and minimize the temptation to spend.
- Debt Management: Carrying high-interest debt might hinder your

financial development. Create a debt repayment strategy, focusing on the highest interest rates initially.
- Investment Strategy: Investing may help your money grow faster than inflation, allowing you to make progress toward your long-term objectives. Investigate several investing choices, such as mutual funds and ETFs, and consider getting expert financial advice depending on your risk tolerance and time frame.

Setting a Course for Financial Freedom

Goal setting and planning are critical components of a safe financial future. You may take charge of your financial future by defining your goals and creating a plan to attain them. This chapter has given you the skills you need to design your own route; nevertheless, keep in mind that your financial journey is continuing. As your circumstances and objectives change, you'll need to examine and alter your strategy accordingly. With a clear goal, a well-defined plan, and a dedication to course corrections, you

Chapter 2: Understanding Your Financial Landscape: Budgeting, Cash Flow, and Net Worth

You've chosen a financial path with certain objectives in mind. Now it's time to comprehend the financial environment you're in. This chapter digs into the principles of financial literacy, providing the tools you need to track your progress and make educated choices.

The Power of Budgeting: Understanding Where Your Money Goes

Imagine starting on a lengthy journey without knowing your fuel capacity or consumption rate. Budgeting plays an important part in your financial path. It is the practice of monitoring your income and costs in order to develop a spending plan that is aligned with your objectives.

Here are some major advantages of budgeting:

- Increased self-awareness: Tracking your expenditure provides useful insights into your financial patterns. Do you underestimate how much you spend dining out? Budgeting helps to discover places where changes may be made.
- Improved financial control: A budget allows you to make mindful spending decisions that are aligned with your objectives. Instead of responding to impulsive cravings, you might set aside cash for your savings objectives.
- Reduced financial stress: Not knowing where your money goes may be a huge cause of worry. Budgeting gives insight and the ability to handle your funds proactively.

Budgeting Methods: Finding the Perfect Fit

There are many budgeting strategies, each with its own set of advantages. Here are some common choices:

- The 50/30/20 Rule: This simple technique directs 50% of your income toward necessities (housing, food, utilities), 30% toward desires (entertainment, eating out), and 20% toward savings and debt reduction.
- The envelope system is a classic approach in which cash is allocated to specified envelopes for various expenditure categories (rent, food, petrol). Once the envelope is empty, spending in that area is halted until the following pay period.
- Zero-Based Budgeting: This strategy allocates every dollar of your income to a defined purpose, such as a cost or a contribution toward a savings goal. This method guarantees that all of your revenue is accounted for and avoids unnecessary expenditure.

Choosing a budgeting approach comes down to personal choice and financial complexity. Regardless matter the strategy, consistency is essential. Track your income and spending on a regular basis, using a budgeting tool, spreadsheet, or pen and paper, depending on what works best for you.

Cash Flow: Understanding Your Income and Outflows

Cash flow is the movement of money into and out of your accounts. It is critical to understand not just how much you make but also how much you spend on a daily basis. Here's what you should consider:

- Income: This comprises your normal wage, any side hustle earnings, and passive income sources (rental income, investment dividends).
- Fixed expenses include known regular expenditures such as rent, mortgage

payments, utilities, insurance fees, and minimum debt payments.
- Groceries, transportation, entertainment, and eating out are examples of variable expenses that change month to month.

Calculating your net cash flow helps you comprehend your financial situation. To do this, deduct your entire costs from your total revenue. A positive cash flow shows that you make more than you spend, while a negative cash flow indicates that you spend more than you earn and may need to change your budget.

Building Your Wealth Compass: Understanding Net Worth

Your net worth is a snapshot of your complete financial situation at a given moment. It is computed by deducting your entire obligations (debts) from your total assets (all you possess with worth). Here's a breakdown:

- Assets include cash, checking and savings account balances, retirement accounts, investments, and the worth of your automobile and house (less any outstanding mortgage).
- Liabilities comprise all of your outstanding bills, such as credit card balances, school loans, vehicle loans, and mortgage amounts.

By measuring your net worth over time, you may measure your progress toward your financial objectives. A growing net worth shows that you are gaining money, but a dropping net worth indicates that you may need to change your spending patterns or look into other revenue sources.

Take Control of Your Financial Journey

Understanding your income, spending, and net worth gives you the ability to make educated financial choices. Budgeting allows you to more efficiently manage your resources, whilst analyzing your cash flow gives critical insights into your financial situation. Mastering these key skills gives you control over your money and empowers you to navigate the thrilling route to your financial objectives.

Chapter 3: Weathering Storms: Risk Management and Protecting Your Future

Life, like any maritime expedition, is never smooth sailing. Unexpected circumstances, like as job loss, sickness, or market downturns, might knock your finances off track. This chapter provides risk management tactics to help you navigate these financial storms and secure your future.

Identifying Your Financial Risks: Understanding Threats

The first stage in risk management is to identify possible hazards. Below are some typical financial risks:

- Market Risk: The value of your assets may vary due to market movements. For example, a stock market catastrophe might damage your retirement assets.

- Credit Risk: A borrower fails on a loan you have granted, resulting in financial loss. Non-payment by renters puts landlords' credit at danger.
- Liquidity risk occurs when you are unable to access your invested money as required owing to market circumstances or investment limitations.
- Inflation Risk: Your money's buying power erodes over time as the cost of goods and services rises. Savings depreciate if not invested to stay up with inflation.
- Longevity Risk: You outlast your retirement resources, which might lead to financial difficulties later in life.
- Disability Risk: An sickness or accident prohibits you from working, limiting your income and capacity to fulfill financial responsibilities.

Building Your Financial Bulwark: Risk Mitigation Strategies

After you've identified possible risks, you may create ways to minimize them.

- Emergency Fund: This critical safety net offers a buffer for unforeseen needs such as auto repairs or medical bills. Aim to save 3-6 months of living costs in an easily accessible account.
- Diversification: Avoid putting all your eggs in one basket. Diversify your assets among asset classes (stocks, bonds, real estate) and industries to mitigate the risk of a single market slump.
- Insurance: Entrust some risks to insurance firms. Consider life insurance to provide for your loved ones in the event of your death, disability insurance to replace income if you are unable to work, and health insurance to cover medical bills.
- Debt Management: Carrying high-interest debt may be a major financial hardship. Create a debt

repayment strategy, beginning with the loans with the highest interest rates. This frees up cash flow and increases your financial freedom.
- Retirement Planning: Begin saving for retirement early and regularly. Use employer-sponsored retirement plans, contribute to IRAs, and create a realistic strategy for replacing your income when you retire.

Create a will and other estate planning papers to guarantee that your assets are dispersed in accordance with your preferences when you die.

Risk Management in Action: A Case Study

Consider John, a young professional with a bright future. He sees job loss as a significant concern. John reduces this risk by establishing a solid emergency fund, updating his résumé, and networking within his field. He also looks into disability insurance to secure his income in the event of a sickness or accident.

Risk management is an ongoing process

Your financial situation will change during your life. As your circumstances change, you should review your risk management techniques on a regular basis. For example, as you near retirement, your risk tolerance for market volatility may decline, forcing changes to your investment portfolio.

Managing Uncertainty with Confidence

Financial risk is an unavoidable fact of life. However, by proactively recognizing possible dangers and employing risk management measures, you may handle these hurdles more confidently. A solid emergency fund, a diverse investment portfolio, and proper insurance coverage create a safety net, enabling you to weather financial storms while staying on track to achieve your objectives. Remember that a well-equipped ship is better prepared to withstand harsh seas, and a solid risk management strategy can help you navigate the uncertainties of the financial voyage.

Chapter 4: Investing for Growth: Selecting the Best Tools and Strategies

Your financial plan is set, and you've filled the ship with necessary supplies (emergency funds and risk management methods). Now is the time to examine the huge investing landscape and arm yourself with the skills you need to increase your wealth and achieve your financial objectives quicker.

Understanding the Power of Investment

Saving is essential for establishing a financial foundation, but it is sometimes insufficient to keep up with inflation and meet long-term objectives such as retirement or a child's education. Investing helps your money to increase quicker than if you kept it in a savings account. Here's how.

- Compound Interest: Albert Einstein described compound interest as the "eighth wonder of the world." It is the interest generated on both the original principle amount invested and the accumulated interest from prior periods. Over time, this compounding impact may greatly increase your wealth.

Exploring the Investment Universe: Asset Classes and Investment Vehicles

The financial world provides a wide range of possibilities, each with its own risk-reward profile. Here's an overview of the main asset classes:

- Stocks: Stocks represent ownership in a firm and have significant development potential, but they also involve a higher risk owing to market volatility.
- Bonds are essentially loans made to a firm or the government that provide regular interest payments and a return

of principle when they mature. They often provide less risk than equities.
- Real estate investments, such as rental houses or commercial buildings, may create income via rent and potentially increase in value. However, real estate has its own set of management obligations.

Investment vehicles consolidate these assets into handy and accessible solutions for investors:

Mutual funds are professionally managed pools of money that invest in a range of assets, providing diversification while minimizing individual stock risk.
- Exchange-Traded Funds (ETFs): Like mutual funds, ETFs are passively managed bundles of assets that trade on stock exchanges all day.

Index funds are mutual funds or ETFs that follow a certain market index and provide wide market exposure with minimal expenses.

Choosing the Right Investment Mix: Creating a Diversified Portfolio

Diversification is the key to a successful investment. Do not put all your eggs in one basket! By diversifying your assets across asset classes and investment vehicles, you mitigate the effect of a single market downturn.

Your appropriate asset allocation is dependent on your risk tolerance, investing objectives, and time horizon.

- Risk Tolerance: How comfortable are you with possible losses? Younger investors with a longer time horizon are more willing to take on risk in exchange for possibly larger profits. As you approach retirement, you may wish to change your portfolio to more conservative assets, such as bonds.

- Investment Goals: Are you saving for a short-term objective, such a down payment on a home, or a long-term goal, such as retirement? Short-term objectives may need a more conservative portfolio, whilst long-term goals might benefit from a greater allocation to growth assets such as equities.
- Time Horizon: How long do you have until you need to retrieve your invested funds? The larger your time horizon, the more risk you may possibly accept, since there is more time to weather market volatility.

Investing Strategies for Different Needs

There are numerous investing techniques based on your objectives and risk tolerance:

- Buy-and-Hold: This long-term approach entails investing in a diverse portfolio and holding it for the foreseeable future, regardless of

short-term market changes. It's ideal for investors with a lengthy time horizon and a low risk tolerance.
- Dollar-Cost Averaging: This method entails investing a certain amount of money in your selected assets on a regular basis, regardless of the current market price. This strategy averages the cost per share across time, lowering the risk of purchasing during a market top.

Seeking professional investment guidance

The investing landscape may be difficult. Consider receiving expert advice from a financial adviser if you are new to investing, have a greater risk tolerance, or have complicated financial objectives. A trained adviser may analyze your risk tolerance, offer appropriate investing methods, and assist you in creating a diversified portfolio that is consistent with your objectives.

Investing in a Brighter Future

Investing is a strong instrument for increasing your wealth and meeting your financial objectives. Understanding the various asset classes, investment vehicles, and diversification methods can allow you to make more educated investing choices. Remember that investing is a marathon, not a sprint. Create a long-term strategy, maintain discipline, and weather market swings with confidence. With the appropriate attitude, you can use the power of investment to guide your financial path to a better future.

Chapter 5: Life's Adventures: Making Big Financial Decisions

Life does not always go as planned. There will be epic experiences, such as purchasing a home, paying off student debt, or planning for retirement, each with its own set of financial challenges. This chapter will help you manage these milestones and keep your financial ship afloat.

1: Homeownership - Finding Your Dream Home

Buying a home is a big decision, but don't allow the enthusiasm cloud your financial judgment. Here's how not to go overboard:

Saving for the Big Splash: Make a 20% down payment to avoid additional expenses. This may require putting some fun money on wait for a time, but your future self will thank you. Explore strategies to increase your savings or start a side job to help you accomplish your goal quicker.

Can You Afford this Ship? Don't only consider the monthly mortgage payment. Consider property taxes, insurance, and unforeseen repairs. A decent rule of thumb is to keep your overall housing expenses below 30% of your income. Consider it an anchor that keeps you on track financially.

be Pre-Approved: Before you begin home looking, be pre-approved for a mortgage. This informs merchants that you are a serious shopper and allows you to keep inside your budget. Imagine attending a treasure hunt without a map - not a good idea, right? Pre-approval is your financial roadmap.

2: Financing Education, Leveling Up Your Skills (and Debt)

Investing in school may have a significant impact, but student debt might seem like a burden. Here are some methods to manage your debt:

Federal loans often offer lower interest rates and greater repayment choices than private loans. Consider these a beginning bundle for your financial education journey.

Scholarships and grants: Free money? Yes, please. Look for scholarships and grants to lower the amount you need to borrow. Every little amount helps to reduce the burden.

Strategic Repayment: Create a strategy to repay such debts efficiently. Consider income-driven repayment programs or debt consolidation to possibly reduce your monthly payments. Remember, this is a marathon, not a sprint. Pace yourself!

3: Retirement Planning - Setting Sail to Relaxation Island

Retirement should be a time to relax and enjoy the results of your effort. Here's how to be financially prepared:

- Start Early - Really Early: The sooner you start saving, the longer your

money has to grow due to compound interest. Even little efforts made early on may have a significant impact in the long run. It's like a snowball moving downhill—the sooner you start, the larger it becomes!
- Employer-Sponsored Booty: Many workplaces will match your retirement plan contributions. That is effectively free money! Contribute as much as you can to claim this prize.
- IRAs: Your Secret Stash: Maximise contributions to IRAs, which provide tax breaks for retirement savings. Imagine it as a hidden pirate treasure filled with riches.

4: Life's Curveballs - Readjusting Your Course

Sometimes life throws us a curveball. Job loss or sickness might have an influence on your financial plans. Here's how to handle the storm:

- Review Your Budget: Take a fresh look at your income and spending. Can you cut out on anything to increase cash flow? Consider tightening the ropes on your sails to negotiate choppy waves.
- Emergency Fund: Your Life Raft: A robust emergency fund serves as a safety net during difficult times. Aim for 3-6 months of living expenditures to stay afloat.
- Be Flexible: If your work security is uncertain, consider setting aside more money for an emergency. The more prepared you are, the smoother the journey.

5: Estate Planning, Leaving Your Legacy

Estate planning guarantees that your belongings are distributed correctly after your death. Here are the necessities.

- A Will: Your Treasure Map: Make a will to specify who inherits your possessions and appoint a guardian for small children. Imagine it as a treasure map for your loved ones.
- Beneficiary Designations: Review who will inherit your retirement assets and life insurance plans. Make sure it is in line with your desires.
- Power of Attorney: If you are unable to handle your financial affairs, delegate authority to someone else. It's like having a reliable first mate to guide the ship if you're unavailable.

Chapter 6: Maintaining Your Course: Monitoring Progress, Re-evaluating, and Making Changes

You've mapped your financial route, armed yourself with the essential tools, and completed some preliminary goals. But a good cruise needs regular monitoring and route modifications. This chapter provides you with the tools you need to track your progress, reevaluate your objectives and methods, and alter your financial plan as required.

- **Monitor Your Progress: Keeping Your Financial Compass Calibrated**

Monitoring your financial success is critical, just as a captain checks his ship's equipment on a regular basis. Here are some important indicators to track:

- Budget Adherence: Are you staying inside your budget? Regularly assess your spending patterns and discover opportunities for improvement.

Budgeting software and spreadsheets may help you see your spending habits and find holes.
- Savings Goals: Are you on pace to meet your short- and long-term savings targets? Calculate your progress on a regular basis and make adjustments to your savings goal as needed. Imagine you're filling a treasure box with riches; monitor your progress to see how full it becomes!
- Investment Performance: How are your investments performing? Review your portfolio on a regular basis and rebalance it if asset allocation deviates from your objective due to market movements. Consider it like examining the sails on your ship to ensure they are correctly set to catch the financial breezes.
- Debt Repayment: Are you making continuous progress towards debt reduction? Track your progress and celebrate accomplishments, such as

paying off a particular credit card. Every debt paid off is a weight removed from your financial anchor.

- **Reevaluating Your Goals: As Life Changes, So Should Your Plan**

Life is a dynamic journey, and your financial objectives will change along the way. Here's why frequent reevaluation is important:

- Life Events: Marriage, children, and work changes all have an influence on your financial requirements and ambitions. After important life events, revisit your strategy to verify that it is still relevant to your present position. Consider it like examining the map: your goal may not change, but the route may need to be adjusted.
- Changing Risk Tolerance: As you age and approach retirement, your risk tolerance may change. To secure your

collected wealth, consider shifting your investing strategy to more conservative investments. Risk tolerance is like ballast on a ship; make sure it's well distributed for a smooth and steady trip.
- Economic Conditions: Market swings and downturns may have an influence on your investment performance and income. Prepare to change your strategy in response to shifting economic conditions. Consider it like sailing during a storm: alter your sails and route as required to keep moving ahead.

- **Making Adjustments: Course Corrections for Smooth Sail**

Prepare to make changes to your financial strategy based on your monitoring and re-evaluation results. Here's how.

- Budget Tweaks: If your spending patterns have changed, alter your budget categories appropriately. Perhaps you could budget more for food or recreation. Remember that a budget is a dynamic document, not something fixed in stone.
- Savings Adjustments: If your short- or long-term objectives have changed, modify your savings contributions appropriately. You may need to save more for a down payment on a property and less for a trip.
- Investment Rebalancing: If your ideal asset allocation has shifted owing to market volatility, rebalance your portfolio to be within your risk tolerance. This might include purchasing or selling assets to meet your goal allocation.

- **Seeking Professional Guidance: When to Hire A Financial Navigator**

Financial planning may be hard. Consult a certified financial planner (CFP) if you:

1. Your financial position is difficult.
2. You have a significant net worth.
3. You are feeling overwhelmed by handling your money. A CFP can provide individualized guidance and assist you with challenging financial choices. Consider them expert navigators who can steer you through unfamiliar financial seas.

A Life-Long Journey - Enjoy It!
Managing your money is a continuous process, not a single event. By frequently assessing your progress, re-evaluating your objectives, and making modifications as appropriate, you guarantee that your financial plan stays in sync with your ever-changing lifestyle. Embrace the voyage, celebrate milestones, and remember that with a well-equipped financial compass and a willingness to make

course adjustments, you have the ability to navigate toward a safe and rewarding financial future. So set sail with confidence and enjoy your financial journey!

www.ingramcontent.com/pod-product-compliance
Lightning Source LLC
Chambersburg PA
CBHW050248230526
45470CB00005B/2165